TRICERATOPS

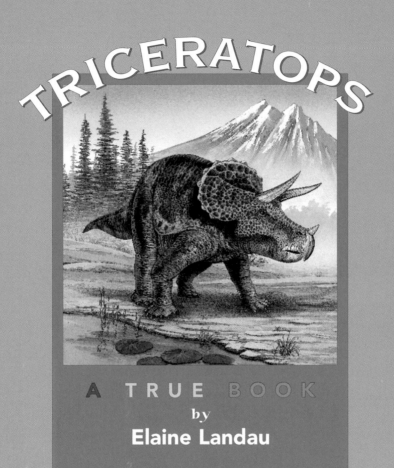

A TRUE BOOK

by

Elaine Landau

Children's Press®
A Division of Grolier Publishing

New York London Hong Kong Sydney
Danbury, Connecticut

Reading Consultant
Linda Cornwell
Coordinator Of School Quality
And Professional Improvement
Indiana State Teachers Association

Science Consultant
Catherine A. Forster
State University of New York
at Stonybrook

Triceratops baby
and adult

Author's Dedication:
For Lana G. Wiess

Visit Children's Press® on the Internet at:
http://publishing.grolier.com

Library of Congress Cataloging-in-Publication Data

Landau, Elaine.
    Triceratops / by Elaine Landau.
        p.   cm. — (A true book)
    Includes bibliographical references (p.   -   ) and index.
    Summary: Describes the characteristics and probable
behavior of this three-horned dinosaur, as well as theories about its
extinction.
    ISBN 0-516-20453-X (lib.bdg.)   0-516-26506-7 (pbk.)
    1. Triceratops—Juvenile literature. [1. Triceratops.
2. Dinosaurs.] I. Title. II. Series.
QE862.065L36   1999   98-8276
567.915'8—dc21   CIP
                                                   AC

Contents

A model of *Triceratops* (top) and a rhinoceros (bottom)

The World of *Triceratops*

Have you ever seen a rhinoceros in a zoo? Perhaps you've seen one in a movie or have seen pictures of these sturdy horned beasts in books. A rhinoceros is not a small animal you could easily miss.

A reconstruction of
Triceratops babies hatching

What if there were an animal that looked something like a rhinoceros, but was much bigger? What if this animal had an even larger head and more horns? Just such an animal once lived. It was a dinosaur known as *Triceratops*.

What is a dinosaur? Dinosaurs were ancient reptiles that lived on land. Like all reptiles, dinosaurs had scaly or leathery skin, lungs, and young that hatched from eggs with shells.

Triceratops roamed the Earth between about 70 million and 65 million years ago. Like all dinosaurs, it lived during the Mesozoic era—a time known as the Age of the Dinosaurs. *Triceratops* appeared toward the end of the Cretaceous period—the last part of the Mesozoic era.

The Earth was very different then from how it is today. It was warmer and there were no cold seasons. Grass didn't exist during the Age of the Dinosaurs. Instead, a blanket of green ferns and other low-growing plants carpeted much

An artist's impression of the landscape during the Late Cretaceous period

of the ground. This was the world of *Triceratops*—one of the last dinosaurs on Earth.

A life-sized model of *Triceratops*

What Did *Triceratops* Look Like?

To get an idea of what *Triceratops* looked like, it may help to picture an overgrown rhinoceros. Like a rhinoceros, *Triceratops* had strong shoulders and a barrel-shaped body.

Of course, *Triceratops* was
much bigger than a rhinoceros.
An adult *Triceratops* was about
30 feet (9 m) long and weighed
between 4 and 6 tons. Some
were even bigger.

Triceratops's massive body was supported by four sturdy legs. Its hind legs were longer than its front ones. However, its short front legs were quite strong. Powerful front limbs were necessary to help support this dinosaur's extremely large head.

Triceratops's head was a full third of its body length. Some of these dinosaurs had skulls that were about 5 feet (1.5 m) long—the height of some adult humans.

It is easy to see why this dinosaur was named *Triceratops*, or "three-horned face." Two long, pointed brow horns jutted out above its eyes. A third shorter horn grew from its nose.

The dinosaur's head was framed by a broad neck frill. This frill was actually a fan-shaped plate of solid bone. It was formed by two large bones growing from behind the animal's skull. Along the

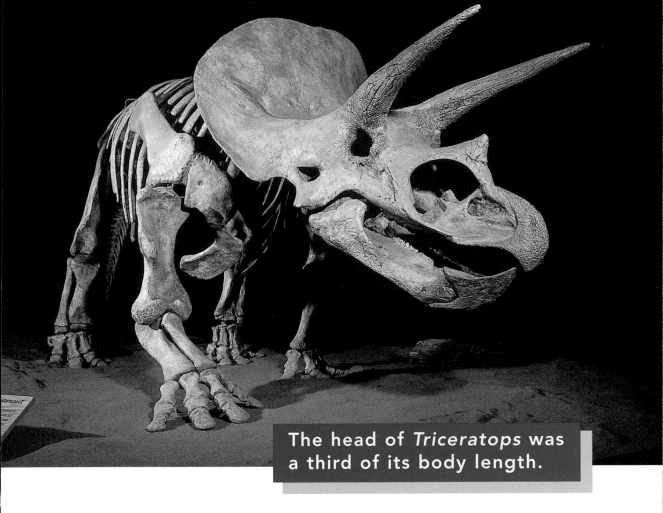

The head of *Triceratops* was a third of its body length.

frill's outer edge was a row of small, pointed, knob-shaped bones.

15

Triceratops had three pointed horns.

Paleontologists—scientists who study prehistoric life—think that *Triceratops* may have used its bony frill as a weapon or shield when other dinosaurs

This view of a *Triceratops* skeleton shows the dinosaur's bony frill.

attacked. Or it may have dis-
played its frill to attract a
mate or frighten off rivals. It
would have lowered its head
to show how big its frill was.

Triceratops was certainly an
impressive beast. It belonged
to a family of dinosaurs called
ceratopsids. Each had a large
head, a bony neck frill, and
horns. *Triceratops* was among
the largest of ceratopsids.

Triceratops had four sturdy legs.

Triceratops ate low-growing plants.

Daily Life

Triceratops was a plant eater. It roamed the land searching for rich, green areas. While looking for food, the dinosaur held its large head close to the ground. It used its horned beak to snatch up plants as well as clumps of leaves and tree branches. *Triceratops* shredded its food with its closely-packed teeth.

A *Triceratops* jawbone

Some researchers think that *Triceratops* might have traveled in herds. This would have provided some protection against predators. Meat-eating dinosaurs would probably have

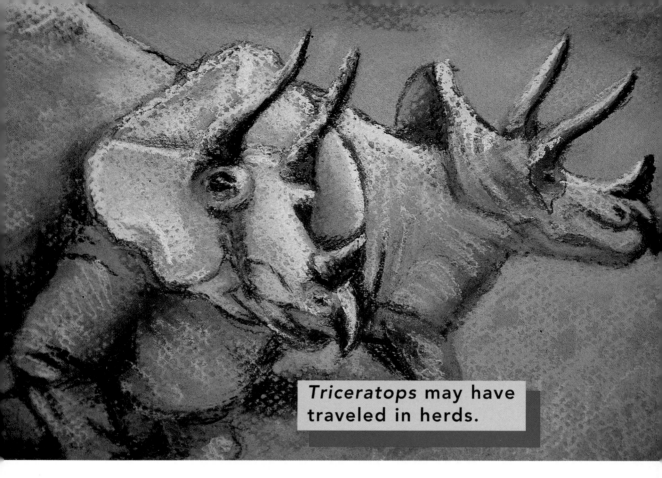

Triceratops may have traveled in herds.

been less likely to attack an entire herd than a single animal. However, no one really knows whether there were herds of *Triceratops*. It's still just a theory.

Triceratops's horns may have been excellent weapons. The bony horns could gorge a predator, wounding or even killing it. *Triceratops* may also have used its horns to fight other *Triceratops* over food or territory.

Triceratops probably used its horns to gorge predators like *Tyrannosaurus rex*.

Finding Fossils

Paleontologists learn about *Triceratops* and other dinosaurs through their fossils. Fossils are the remains of animals and plants that have been buried in the Earth's crust for thousands or millions of years. Over time, these remains, as well as the soil they were buried in, turn to rock.

A dinosaur fossil
imbedded in rock

Most fossils are uncovered through erosion—when rain, rivers, and wind wear down the rock and expose the buried fossils. In rare cases, fossils have been found after rock deposits have been blasted apart for industry.

Dinosaur researchers also learn from fossil footprints. These are formed when a prehistoric animal leaves a footprint in the mud and then the mud, over a very long time, hardens into rock. Through a dinosaur's fossil footprint, researchers can learn how large the animal was.

Triceratops fossils have been located in the United States in Montana, North Dakota, South Dakota, and Wyoming. In Canada, Triceratops fossils have been found in Alberta and Saskatchewan.

A view of the back of a *Triceratops* skeleton

A Wrong Guess

The first triceratops fossil found was a set of brow horns. But when famous paleontologist O. C. Marsh examined it in 1887, he thought the horns belonged to an extinct bison. He didn't learn until two years later that horned dinosaurs existed.

ALBERTA

SASKATCHEWAN

MANITOBA

CANADA

UNITED STATES

Area of Detail

MINNESOTA

NORTH DAKOTA

SOUTH DAKOTA

MONTANA

IDAHO

WYOMING

IOWA

NEBRASKA

VADA

UTAH

COLORADO

KANSAS

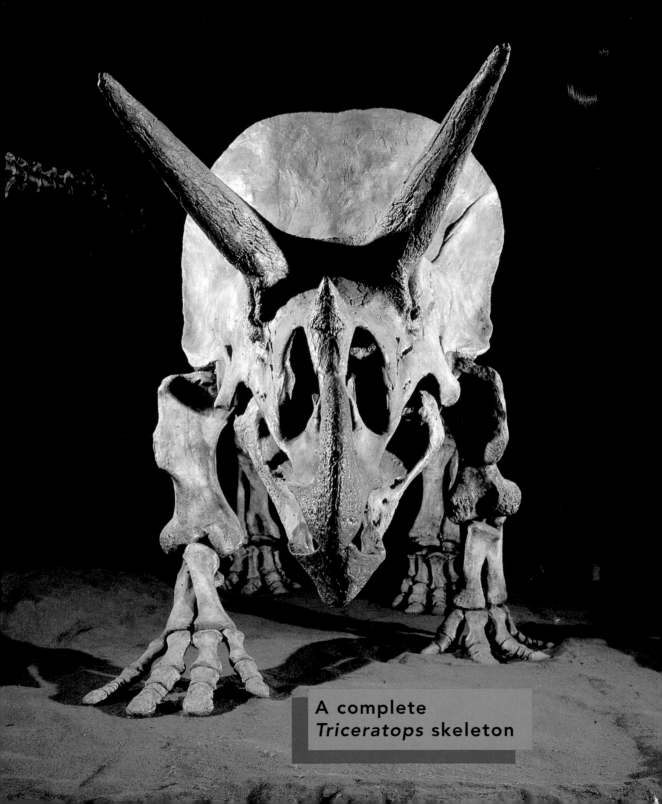

A complete
Triceratops skeleton

The Dinosaur Disappearance

Do you think that all dinosaurs became extinct at the same time? If so, you are only partly right. For about 150 million years, various kinds of dinosaurs existed. Yet no single type of dinosaur lasted for that entire time. Most species of dinosaurs lasted on Earth for only a few million years.

Scientists aren't sure why different dinosaurs died out when they did.

But at the end of the Cretaceous period, all the remaining dinosaurs–as well as most other living creatures

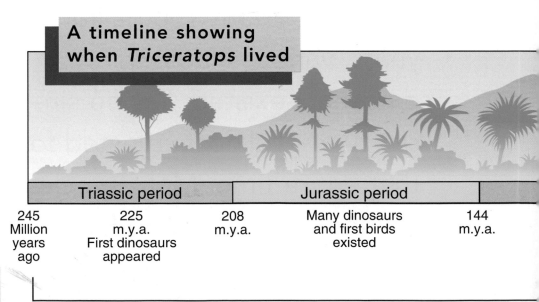

A timeline showing when *Triceratops* lived

Triassic period	Jurassic period	

| 245 Million years ago | 225 m.y.a. First dinosaurs appeared | 208 m.y.a. | Many dinosaurs and first birds existed | 144 m.y.a. |

Mesozoic era

on Earth—died out. Even this didn't happed in one day, but over a period of about a million years. Researchers don't know for sure what caused this mass extinction. The two most likely theories are described below.

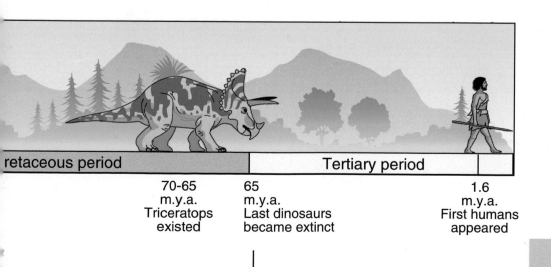

retaceous period	Tertiary period	
70-65 m.y.a. Triceratops existed	65 m.y.a. Last dinosaurs became extinct	1.6 m.y.a. First humans appeared

An artist's impression of a dinosaur seeing a comet heading towards Earth

One theory is that the dinosaurs became extinct after a comet or asteroid crashed into Earth. Comets and asteroids are large bodies that move through space. If a comet or asteroid struck Earth, a tremendous crater would be created. The dust from the hole would float up into the atmosphere. The dust particles would form thick, dark clouds blocking out the Sun.

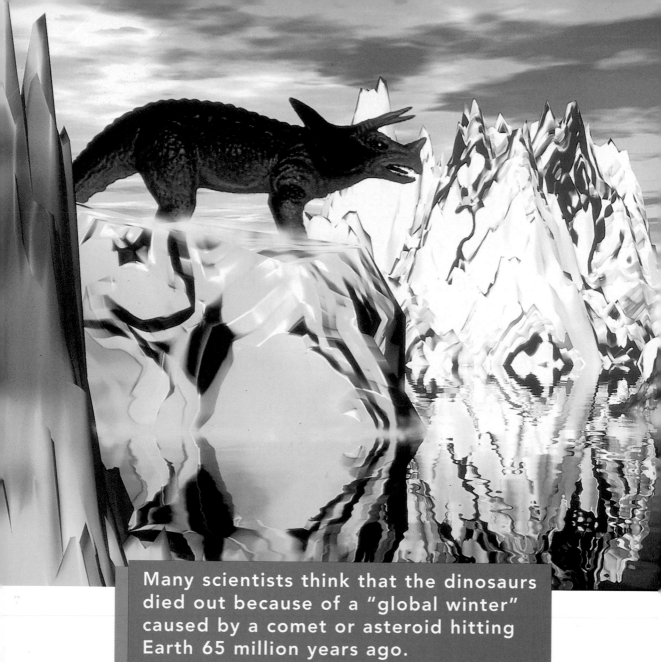

Many scientists think that the dinosaurs died out because of a "global winter" caused by a comet or asteroid hitting Earth 65 million years ago.

Without sunlight, the weather on Earth would have become quite cold. Some researchers believe dinosaurs could not have survived in such a climate.

Another theory is that environmental change caused the extinction of the dinosaurs. Throughout the Age of the Dinosaurs, the world was changing continually. Large land areas were splitting apart to form continents.

A student digging
for dinosaur fossils

Seas and mountain ranges were taking shape as well. As the climate cooled, different types of plant life appeared. Some think that when the dinosaurs could no longer adapt to these changes, they died out.

We may never know exactly what happened to the dinosaurs. *Triceratops* vanished toward the end of the Cretaceous period along with the rest of these animals.

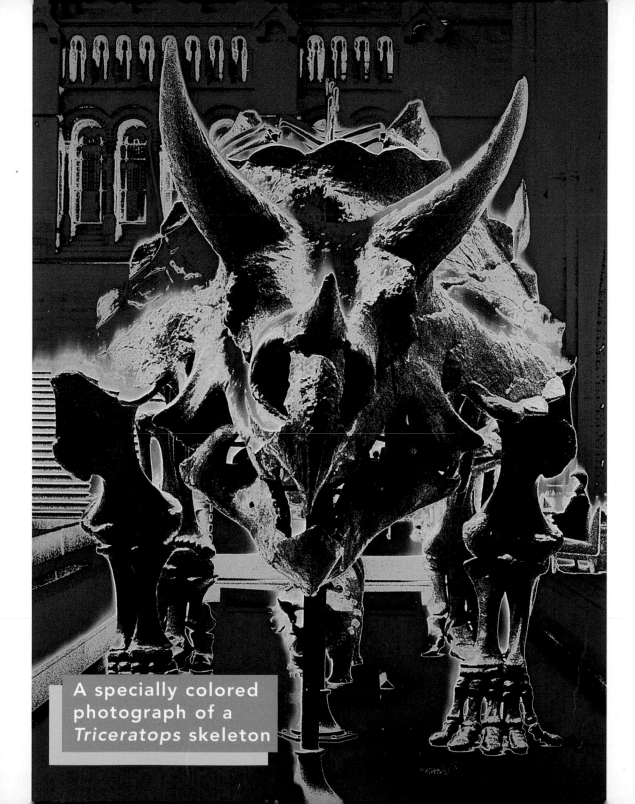

A specially colored photograph of a *Triceratops* skeleton

Luckily, a large number of well-preserved *Triceratops* fossils have been found in North America. Through these, paleontologists have pieced together what this sturdy, three-horned dinosaur was like.

To Find Out More

Here are some additional resources to help you learn more about *Triceratops:*

Books

Amazing Dinosaurs: the Fastest, the Smallest, the Fiercest, and the Tallest. Western Publishing Company, 1991.

Arnold, Caroline. **Dinosaurs Around the World: An Artist's View of the Prehistoric World.** Clarion Books, 1993.

Benton, Michael J. **How Do We Know Dinosaurs Existed?** Raintree Steck-Vaughn, 1995.

Brenner, Barbara. **Dinosaurium.** Bantam Books, 1993.

Henderson, Douglas. **Dinosaur Tree.** Bradbury Press, 1994.

Lauber, Patricia. **Living with Dinosaurs.** Bradbury Press, 1991.

Lindsay, William. **Triceratops.** Dorling Kindersley, 1993.

Most, Bernard. **How Big Were the Dinosaurs?** Harcourt Brace & Co., 1994.

Mullins, Patricia. **Dinosaur Encore.** Harper Collins, 1993.

Pringle, Laurence. **Dinosaurs! Strange and Wonderful.** Boyds Mills Press, 1995.

American Museum of Natural History
Central Park West at
79th Street
New York, NY 10024
http://www.amnh.org

One of the world's largest natural-history museums, with exceptional collections on dinosaurs and fossils. Its website has a special *Triceratops* page.

DinoDon.com
http://www.DinoDon.com

Includes dinosaur art, a dinosaur dictionary, dinosaur news, and information on contests, digs, scientists, books, and links.

Dinorama
*http://www.
nationalgeographic.com/
dinorama/frame.html*

A *National Geographic* site with information about dinosaurs and current methods of learning about them. Includes timelines, animations, and fun facts.

National Museum of Natural History, Smithsonian Institution
10th Street and
Constitution Ave. NW
Washington, D.C. 20560
*http://www.mnh.si.edu/
nmnhweb.html*

In the museum's Dinosaur Hall, you can see—and in one case touch—real fossils of dinosaurs.

ZoomDinosaurs
*http://www.
ZoomDinosaurs.com/*

A site that contains everything you might want to know about dinosaurs and other ancient reptiles. Its *Triceratops* page includes facts, myths, activities, a geologic time chart, printouts, and links.

Important Words

adapt to adjust to

asteroid rocky, planetlike object orbiting in space

atmosphere layer of gases surrounding the Earth

comet frozen ball of water, gases, and dust from the farthest reaches of our solar system

extinct no longer in existence

imbedded stuck into

gorge stab

predator animal that hunts other animals for food

prehistoric before recorded history

remains bones, teeth, or tissue left behind after a plant or animal dies

Index

Meet the Author

Elaine Landau has a Bachelor of Arts degree in English and Journalism from New York University and a Master's degree in Library and Information Science from Pratt Institute. She has worked as a newspaper reporter, children's book editor, and a youth-services librarian, but especially enjoys writing for young people.

Ms. Landau has written more than one hundred nonfiction books on various topics. She lives in Miami, Florida, with her husband, Norman, and son, Michael.

Photographs ©: Ben Klaffke: 2 (Drawing by L. Stevens), 4 top, 10, 12, 16, 17, 22, 23, 26, 29, 30, 40; Corbis-Bettmann: 19; Photo Researchers: 24 (Chris Butler/SPL), 15, 32 (Francois Gohier), 4 bottom (Philip Kahl), 6, 20 (Tom McHugh), 9 (Ludek Pesek/SPL), 36 (Mike Agliolo Productions), 38 (Victor Habbick Visions/ SPL), 42 (Sinclair Stammers/SPL).
Illustrations by Greg Harris
Maps by Bob Italiano